For Virginia

Published 2007 by Raven Productions, Inc.
P.O. Box 188, Ely, MN 55731
(218) 365-3375 www.ravenwords.com

Text and illustration © 1995 by Consie Powell
Originally published by Roberts Rinehart Publishers.

Library of Congress Cataloging-in-Publication Data

Powell, Consie.
  A bold carnivore : an alphabet of predators / Consie
Powell.
      p. cm.
  Originally published: Niwot, Colo. : Roberts Rinehart .
c1995.
  ISBN 978-0-9766264-8-0 (hardcover : alk. paper) --
ISBN 978-0-9766264-9-7 (pbk. : alk. paper)
  1. Predatory animals--North America--Juvenile
literature. 2. Alphabet books. I. Title.
  QL758.P68 2007
  591.5'3--dc22

                                            2007009613

Printed in Manitoba
Canada
10 9 8 7 6 5 4 3 2 1

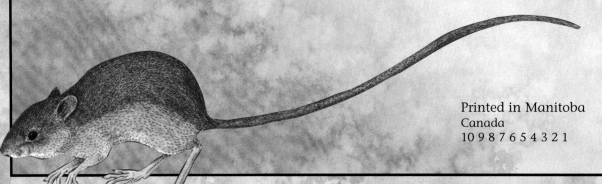

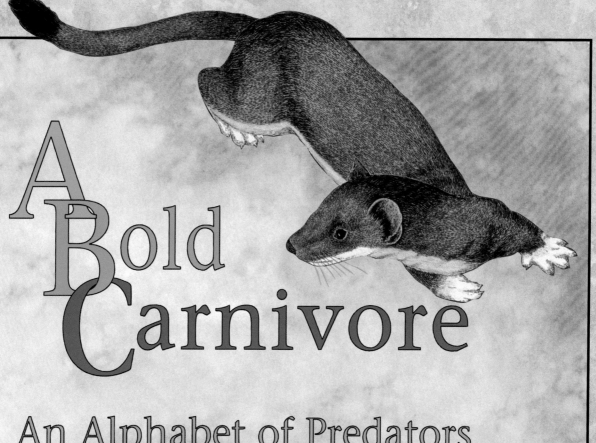

A Bold Carnivore

An Alphabet of Predators

Consie Powell

Raven Productions, Inc. Ely, Minnesota

This is a book about predators and their prey. Each letter of the alphabet introduces a different North American predator. Surrounding each predator are illustrations of a variety of its prey.

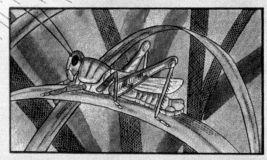

All living creatures
   must eat to survive.
Some eat plants;
   others eat those who eat the plants.
All are links in the
   great food chain of life.

These are predators,
   large or small, furred, feathered,
   smooth or scaly skinned.

Some search, some chase, but
   all want to catch a meal.
Some watch, some hide, for
   some might become a meal.

A a

Alligator

Floating like a fallen log, an alligator waits to grab an unsuspecting muskrat.

B b

Bat

On paper-thin wings of delicate leather, a little brown bat flutters through the night and catches flying insects.

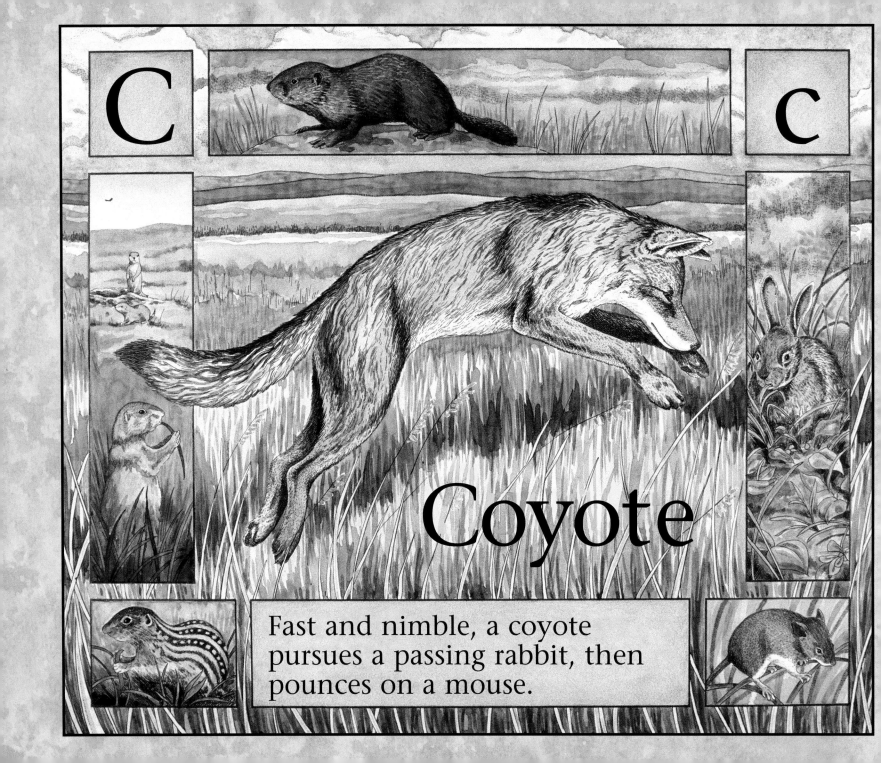

C c

Coyote

Fast and nimble, a coyote pursues a passing rabbit, then pounces on a mouse.

D d

Damselfly

A damselfly dips and darts through the summer air, catching mosquitoes and midges.

E e

Elf owl

When night falls, a tiny elf owl wakes and hunts the cool desert for small rodents or large insects.

F f

Fisher

A fisher searches the deep woods for hares or squirrels; the porcupine is safe up in a tree.

G g

Grass spider

When an insect vibrates the funnel-shaped web, a grass spider dashes out to capture its prey.

H h

Hawk

A broad-winged hawk patiently waits and watches for movement of a mouse, frog, or snake.

I i

Ibis

A white-faced ibis probes its long, curved bill underwater for minnows or tiny crayfish.

J j

Jellyfish

A jellyfish floats on soft ocean swells as it waits to tangle and stun a fish in its long tentacles.

K   k

Kingsnake

An eastern kingsnake hunts along stream banks for turtle eggs or water snakes.

L l

Lynx

Alone and quiet, a lynx stalks through the northern forest in pursuit of a snowshoe hare.

M m

Merganser

A hungry merganser pops to the surface. Only fish, frogs, or crayfish that hide carefully escape this diving duck.

N n

Newt

A slippery red-spotted newt searches a quiet stream bottom for leeches or frog eggs.

O o

Orca

In its ocean world, a sleek orca hunts for seals, fish, and floating sea birds.

P p

Pelican

A big brown pelican flies or floats, and always watches for fish to catch in its deep-pouched bill.

Q q

Quail

Young quail feast on ants, beetles, and crickets to help them grow into strong adults.

R r

Ringtail

An eager ringtail prowls the dark desert in search of a mouse, bird, or lizard.

S S

Shrew

A little short-tailed shrew feeds almost constantly on worms, snails, and insects just to stay alive.

T t

Toad

In the soft spring twilight, a hungry toad snaps up flies, earthworms and slugs.

U u

Uta

Over a tumble of desert boulders, an uta lizard prowls in search of insects and mites.

V v

Veery

A veery sings a gentle flute-like song. It gulps down a fat caterpillar with gusto.

W   W

Weasel

Bold and curious, a hungry long-tailed weasel snoops and sniffs in search of a mouse or vole.

X   X

mureX

A frill-wing murex snail bores its rasping tongue into a living clam's shell, then eats the clam inside.

Yellow perch

In a freshwater lake, yellow perch swim in search of smaller fish and insect larvae.

Z

Zapus

A Zapus eats seeds and insects when it can catch them. This mouse escapes other predators with a huge jump.

Glossary

Prey shown for each predator are listed in clockwise order, starting at the top.

A: Alligator

American alligators inhabit freshwater swamps, bayous, lakes, and slow rivers in the southeastern United States. They can survive weeks without eating but grow rapidly if they eat frequently.

PREY SHOWN: muskrat, great blue heron, bluegill, beaver, mallards.

B: Bat

Little brown bats live in colonies near water or forests throughout most of North America except the southernmost areas. Those that live far north migrate south in autumn to hibernate.

PREY SHOWN: spotted cutworm moth, striped cutworm moth, zebra caterpillar moth, mosquitoes, Zabulon skipper, Isabella moth, hog sphinx moth, cottonwood dagger moth.

C: Coyote

Adaptable hunters, coyotes populate all parts of the continent. A pounce through tall grasses catches a vole or mouse by pinning it beneath the forepaws.

PREY SHOWN: woodchuck, cottontail rabbit, western harvest mouse, thirteen-lined ground squirrel, black-tailed prairie dogs.

D: Damselfly

Damselflies live near ponds, marshes, or lakes throughout North America. After hatching, damselfly nymphs molt as many as 15 times before developing into adults.

PREY SHOWN: black flies, eastern floodwater mosquitoes, black fly, salt-marsh mosquito, midges.

E: Elf owl

No bigger than a sparrow, the nocturnal elf owl inhabits desert lowlands, canyons, and foothills in the arid southwestern United States and Mexico. It often nests in saguaro cactus.

PREY SHOWN: centipede, millipede, kangaroo rat, scorpion, polyphemus moth, desert pocket mouse.

F: Fisher

A fisher is a solitary hunter in mixed hardwood forests across Canada and the far northern United States. It will catch a porcupine only if it can bite the quill-less face.

PREY SHOWN: red squirrel, snowshoe hare, spruce grouse, deer mouse, porcupine.

G: Grass spider

The web of a grass spider is not sticky, but instead acts as a "telegraph" to alert the spider to prey. Found throughout North America, grass spiders depend on speed to catch their food.

PREY SHOWN: green lacewing, four-lined plant bug, boxelder bug, gladiator katydid, bilobed looper caterpillar, firefly, scarlet and green leafhopper, crane fly.

H: Hawk

Broad-winged hawks dwell in coniferous and deciduous forests in central and eastern North America. They hunt by perching to watch for prey. In autumn they migrate by the thousands to South America.

PREY SHOWN: deer mouse, eastern garter snake, American toad, differential grasshopper, leopard frog.

I: Ibis

White-faced ibises feed and nest in swamps and sloughs of the great plains states. They usually share these sites with other wading birds.

PREY SHOWN: leopard frog, crayfish, speckled dace minnows, predacious water beetle larvae, tadpoles.

J: Jellyfish

Found in oceans all over the world, jellyfish are not fish at all. This purple jellyfish is related to sea anemones and corals because they all have jellylike bodies, tentacles, and stinging cells to immobilize prey.

PREY SHOWN: striped anchovies, blackbar soldierfish, flamefish, tattler, horned krill.

K: Kingsnake

Eastern kingsnakes live in the southeastern United States. Other kingsnakes live throughout the United States and parts of Mexico: all are immune to the venoms of poisonous snakes they eat.

PREY SHOWN: northern water snake, meadow vole, green anole, ovenbird, five-lined skink.

L: Lynx

Hunting and living alone, lynxes range widely through forests and scrub in Alaska, Canada, and northern wilds of the lower 48 states. Their large hairy paws act as snowshoes in winter.

PREY SHOWN: snowshoe hare (winter), snowshoe hare (summer), spruce grouse, tundra vole, red squirrel.

M: Merganser

On freshwater lakes across northern North America, common mergansers dive and hunt. Toothlike edges on their bills help the birds hold onto prey.

PREY SHOWN: bullfrog, crayfish, tadpoles, campeloma snail, yellow perch.

N: Newt

Red-spotted newts live in temperate climates in eastern North America. A newt larva hatches from an egg in water, then develops into a "red eft" and lives on land. Upon reaching adulthood, the newt lives primarily in water again.

PREY SHOWN: frog eggs, tadpoles, crayfish, leeches, earthworm, waterstrider.

O: Orca

Orcas live and hunt in family groups in cold waters of the Pacific and Atlantic oceans. Orcas hunting fish signal one another with whistles and clicks; those hunting mammals hunt silently.

PREY SHOWN: south polar skua, thick-billed murre, harbor porpoise, squid, chinook salmon, California sea lion.

P: Pelican

Brown pelicans fish in salt water on the Pacific, Atlantic, and Gulf coasts. As they hunt, pelicans often fly so close to the water that their wings almost brush the waves.

PREY SHOWN: shiner perch, Pacific sardines, garibaldi, striped sea perch, rubberlip sea perch.

Q: Quail

Adult California quail are primarily seed eaters. They occupy open woodlands near water along the west coast of the United States and Baja California.

PREY SHOWN: cornfield ants, creosote bush grasshopper, western subterranean termite, field cricket, California checkered beetle.

R: Ringtail

Nocturnal ringtails live in dry, rocky areas of the southwestern United States and Mexico, and occasionally eat fruit as well as animal prey. They are distantly related to coatis and raccoons.

PREY SHOWN: kangaroo rat, zebra-tailed lizard, desert pocket mouse, desert tarantula, cactus wren.

S: Shrew

Short-tailed shrews inhabit woods and moist areas in southeastern Canada and the central and northeastern United States. Because a shrew must eat at least every 3 hours, it is active day and night.

PREY SHOWN: weevil grubs, downy leatherwing beetle, springtail, aphids, earthworms, field cricket, snail, southeastern lubber grasshopper.

T: Toad

American toads, found in central and eastern United States and Canada, may reside in suburban backyards or pristine wilderness. They need shallow water to breed and moist hiding places to rest and to hunt.

PREY SHOWN: earthworm, toxomerus hover fly, tree-hole mosquitoes, flower beetle larvae, slug.

U: Uta

Uta lizards are abundant in arid western North America. These small lizards have a dark blotch behind each foreleg and are sometimes called side-blotched lizards.

PREY SHOWN: daddy-longlegs, sowbugs, Mormon cricket, cactus fly, velvet mites.

V: Veery

The shy veery dwells in dense, moist woodlands along the United States-Canada border and the Rocky Mountains. Though secretive and seldom seen, its lively song betrays its presence.

PREY SHOWN: forest tent caterpillar, red and blue checkered beetle, earthworm, bush katydid, little sulphur caterpillar.

W: Weasel

At least one of the three species of weasels (long-tailed, short-tailed, and least weasels) is found anywhere in North America. Northern weasels turn white in winter, while southern weasels stay brown.

PREY SHOWN: meadow vole, deer mouse, red-backed vole, chipmunk, zapus mouse.

X: mureX

Frill-wing murexes inhabit underwater rocks and crevices along the coast of California. Some may be exposed at low tide, but others inhabit deeper coastal waters.

PREY SHOWN: Kelsey's date mussel, California cumingia clam, Peruvian jingle shell, clear jewel box, native Pacific oyster.

Y: Yellow perch

Schools of yellow perch populate clear, cold streams and lakes across central and eastern Canada and the United States. They feed in shallow and deep waters at dawn and dusk.

PREY SHOWN: emerald shiner, dragonfly and mayfly larvae, log perch, midge and mosquito larvae, water boatmen.

Z: Zapus

A Zapus, also known as a meadow jumping mouse, hides by day and feeds at night. Zapus are found in northern habitats, and hibernate during winter.

PREY SHOWN: rose weevil, spotted cutworm caterpillar, fiery searcher beetle, fragile ground beetle, buffalo grass seeds.